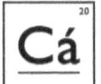

CÁNTARO **Cá** LIBRARY

MARTIN LUTHER
& THE 95 THESES

CARL E. KOPPENHAVER

Foreword by Steven R. Martins

Dedicated to the faithful readership of the Cántaro Institute

cántaro
publications

cantaroinstitute.org

Martin Luther & the 95 Theses
Published by Cántaro Publications, a publishing imprint of
Cántaro Institute, Jordan Station, ON.

Martin Luther by Carl E. Koppenhaver, originally published
1953, by Muhlenberg Press.

*Disputation of Doctor Martin Luther on the Power and Efficacy
of Indulgences* by Martin Luther, originally published in Latin,
1517, and translated and edited by Adolph Spaeth, L.D. Reed,
Henry Eyster Jacobs, et. al., as it was published in 1915 by the
A. J. Holman Company.

ISBN: 978-1-990771-40-8

Printed in the United States of America

CONTENTS

FOREWORD

IN THE YEAR 1517, a German monk named Martin Luther (1483–1546) nailed to the church door in Wittenburg his 95 Theses.[1] This was not some easy-to-read tract, nor was it written as a treatise for the common people, it was instead written as an academic dispute against what the Roman Catholic Church was teaching at the time, principally concerning the sale of indulgences – or to put this in more simpler terms, *paying your way* (and that of your relatives) *to heaven.*

Apparently, according to the papacy, it had not been enough that Jesus died on the cross for man's sin, man had to do something *in addition* to such a costly work by the Christ. And the fact that man had to *pay* the church – as a means to make up for that insufficiency of Christ's work

---

1. See Michael Reeves, *The Unquenchable Flame: Discovering the Heart of the Reformation*, Kindle Edition (Nashville, TN.: B&H Publishing, 2009).

– severely upset Luther. Why did this provoke such consternation? Because the sale of indulgences stands in plain contradiction to what the Word of God teaches concerning the redemptive work of the Christ and the doctrine of salvation in general.

The Context

One needs to bear in mind that, at the time, the common people did not have access to a Bible. And this meant that they were easily manipulated given that the Scriptures were kept in hiding so to speak. It was not a matter of simply obtaining a copy of the Scriptures, but *understanding* it. The Scriptures were hidden in the sense that they were restricted to their respective ancient languages, that of Hebrew, Greek, and Latin, and to have it translated into the vernacular was prohibited. Even if a commoner were to have hypothetically held a Bible in their hands (which was the dream of the reformers), they would not have been able to read it unless they had studied at the Roman Catholic academic institutions. And an education in the ancient languages would have been included, along with a wagon-load of Catholic indoctrination. Luther, however, *had* studied the Scriptures, and he was troubled by what he had found.

What troubled this devout Catholic monk, which for the most part had been docile and submissive to the church? That what the Word of God had to say was not at all what the Roman Catholic Church had been teaching. There were two "Gods" being pitted against each other, the God of Scripture, and the God of Roman Catholicism. Which was the true God? It does not require much effort on our part to answer, "the God of Scripture", but in the sixteenth-century, the people mostly knew the God of Romanism, and had no choice but to take the Catholic priest at his word. It is within this historical context that we see this contention between what Luther discovered and what the pope declared to be truth.

If you really want to appreciate the magnitude of this contention, it would do you well to understand Luther's background story, because the story of his life has, in fact, a great deal to do with his strong disagreement with Romanism's soteriology. This is one of the reasons why we have decided to republish Carl E. Koppenhaver's *Martin Luther*, which summarizes clearly what God in His divine providence brought about for the good of His church. In truth, what Luther accomplished by nailing those 95 Theses was to start a movement, albeit not intentionally, that would forever change the world. That movement was the recovery of the gospel, the recovery of biblical truth, and that movement had been made possible due to the efforts of several "outlaws" across Europe who made every effort to translate the Bible into the common tongue, even under the severe threat and penalty of death.

Luther was one of those men, he translated the Bible into German, while in England it was William Tyndale (d. 1536) who translated it into English,[2] and in Spain, Casiodoro de Reina (1520–1594) who translated it into Spanish, with a later revision by Cipriano de Valera (1531–1602).[3] Of course, there were several others, but it suffices for now to mention these few.

It is difficult to imagine what it would have been like to read the Bible in one's own language

---

2.   See David Teems, *Tyndale: The Man Who Gave God an English Voice* (Nashville, TN.: Thomas Nelson, 2012).

3.   See Manuel Diaz Pineda, *La Reforma en España (Siglos XVI-XVIII): Origen, naturaleza y creencias* (Barcelona, España: Editorial Clie, 2017); *Casiodoro de Reina: Ensayos en honor del 500 aniversario de su nacimiento*, ed. Andrés Messmer (Barcelona, España: Editorial Clie, 2023).

for the very first time, after *years* of being shown
a false image of who God really is. Luther, for
example, thought God was evil, capricious, and
cruel, because He supposedly gave man nothing
more than a set of laws that no man could possibly
fulfill in its fullness, but that false image was the
byproduct of Romanism.

With the introduction of such things as purgatory, the acquisition of relics, the good deeds
done to outweigh the bad, the money given in
hopes of gaining favour with God, the prayers to
the saints, etc., what Luther essentially saw, like
many like him, was the "God" according to the
fallen image of man. But when Luther read the
Scriptures for himself, he was not afraid of what
would come upon him from such a false image,
and this was because he had found the answers to
his questions, he had found the true God in the
text of the Christian Scriptures, a God who was
not evil, capricious, or cruel. He found instead
a God of love, of mercy, of grace – not divorced
from His absolute righteousness and holiness[4] –
he found a God worth dying for, and Luther almost
did.

---

4.   See *Martin Luther: Selections from his Writings*, ed.
     John Dillenberger (New York, NY.: Anchor Books,
     1962).

Luther, along with other reformers during his time, such as John Calvin, Ulrich Zwingli, Pierre Viret, etc., would go on to contribute towards the recovery of five biblical principles, which we know today as the five *Solas*, that we are: "Saved by Grace alone (*Sola Gratia*), through Faith alone (*Sola Fide*), in Christ alone (*Solus Christos*), according to Scripture alone (*Sola Scriptura*), for the Glory of God alone (*Soli Deo Gloria*)." These biblical, doctrinal truths were discovered by the reformers as they set out to read Scripture with minds unhitched from the corruption of Romanism; it was as if they were receiving the Gospels, or the New Testament letters, directly from the first-century authors themselves. You can just imagine the excitement and the wonder. Perhaps even the disdain over how the church had fallen and strayed into apostasy.

The question, of course, that has always lingered historically has been, Why did the Roman Catholic Church have a problem with the terms "grace", "faith", "Christ", "Scripture", or "the glory of God"? The answer to that question can be complex to a certain degree when one bears in mind the difference of religious worldviews, but a short answer will suffice for the time being by simply stating that the answer is not to be found in the biblical terms themselves, because these terms have been used and interpreted according to the established dogma of Romanism. Instead, the contention is in the addition of the word "alone", which was what the reformers emphasized as they sought to break with Romanism's eisegesis (reading into the text) and return to biblical exegesis (having the text speak for itself). This is what Romanism could not stand, and what the reformers taught: Salvation by grace *alone*, through faith *alone*, in Jesus Christ *alone*, according to Scripture *alone*, for the glory of God *alone*. This may be an over-simplification of the five *Solas*,[5] but it sufficiently provides you with a surface-level understanding. The reformers were essentially calling the church back to the truth of God's inscripturated revelation. And there were several before Luther who sounded the alarm only to be snuffed out by the Roman Catholic authorities who wanted not a soul to question the authority and power of the pope and the institution he presided over. But when Luther came on the scene, the conditions were ripe across Europe for a movement to begin, for the church to recover

---

5.   See *Sola: How the Five Solas Are Still Reforming the Church*, ed. Jason K. Allen and et al (Chicago, IL. Moody Publishers, 2019).

the biblical gospel, to recover the biblical principles of the *Solas*, and while the reformation is far greater than Luther himself, we cannot turn a blind eye to the courage of a German monk who was willing to lay his life down for the truth of God's Word, and who hence served as a providential catalyst. And what a catalyst he was.

Luther's Life Story

Prior to Luther's nailing of the 95 Theses, and prior to his contributions to the protestant reformation, Luther was an insignificant monk who worked tirelessly to make up for his many sins. Each time he sinned he spent increasingly more time in confession, and because of every sin he confessed, his confessors are said to have grown tired with his confessions lasting long hours.[6] You could probably imagine Luther recounting hour after hour every sin that occurred to him, sin after sin after sin without cease, and it was not hard to do. If we were to look at our own lives and judge our hearts according to the perfection demanded by God's law, how many faults would you find in yourself? A man who knows himself well is a man who knows himself to be a most wretched sinner, because he *knows*

---

6. Reeves, *The Unquenchable Flame*, 38-39.

the multitude of his sins. And we could perhaps imagine Luther's confessor, the priest who was assigned to listen to him, falling asleep as a result of these long hours of confession, perhaps even secretly praying that God would take the man or he would send him up there to heaven himself. But as Luther would discover, with his study of Scripture, God is nothing like the priests of fallen men. God does not tire to hear from man, in fact, He invites men and women like us to unceasing prayer, to continual repentance, and to restored fellowship in the Son. Contrary to the teachings of Romanism, God's grace is not earned nor bought, it is freely given as a gift. And His words of grace are nothing like the words of peace that are offered by a priest, those are nothing but empty words that mean nothing in the sight of God and provide no consolation. God's grace brings peace to our hearts precisely because we see the goodness of the Law, and how God has provided the means by which we can live according to the Law, *by His grace alone through faith alone in the Son alone, according to His Word alone, for the glory of God alone.*

You will notice that enclosed in this publication we have provided an English translation of the 95 Theses. While the academic disputation, originally written in Latin by Luther, is one which must be understood within its historical context, it is nonetheless a historical document that every Christian should acquaint themselves with in order to be familiarized with our protestant heritage, as well as reminded as to how God can providentially use that which appears to be insignificant or irrelevant for His most glorious ends. And as we look upon God's church today, and what the reformation has brought about, and the reformation spirit that still lives within us, we have no other fitting words to say other than *Soli Deo Gloria.*

1

THE MINER'S SON

1.1 Eisleben to Erfurt

THE TURK WAS SLASHING his way up the valley
of the Danube into the heart of Europe. God sat
far off, not as a loving father but as a vengeful
law-court judge inflicting all sorts of misery on
mankind. In the forest lurked witches and de-
mons seeking to drag the unwary to destruction.

Into such a world threatened by the sword,
ruled by fear, and plagued by superstition,
Martin Luther was born on November 10, 1483,
in Eisleben, Germany. Within such a world he
became a man disdainful of bodily harm, convinced of God's love and mercy, endowed with
abundant common sense—a Christian worthy
of study and emulation. Although his station of
birth was lowly, greatness sought him out, and the
whole world has felt the impact of his life.

The Luther child was baptized in the Church
of St. Peter the morning after his birth and was

named Martin for the saint of the day. His parents, Hans and Margarethe Luther, were simple, industrious folk. They had moved recently from the farming community of Möhra, home of the Luther family, to Eisleben where Hans hoped to make his fortune in the copper mines.

When Martin was about six months old the family moved to near-by Mansfeld. The first years there were hard and it was with difficulty that Hans scraped together money to send his son to school. By the time Martin was thirteen, however, his father was able to send him to a school conducted by the Brothers of the Common Life at Magdeburg. As was the custom, he earned his board by singing and begging from door to door with one of the school choirs.

He stayed in Magdeburg for only a year and then was sent to the parish school of St. George in Eisenach. While again earning his keep by singing and begging, he became acquainted with Frau Ursula Cotta, a woman of culture and refinement, who took the promising young scholar into her home.

Hans Luther had been working diligently and by the time his son was seventeen the family budget permitted his entrance to the University of Erfurt. Martin worked diligently too, and at the end of four years had passed not only his bachelor's but his master's examinations.

1.2 Into the Cloister

Obedient to his father's wishes, Martin Luther on May 20, 1505, began his post-graduate studies at Erfurt, preparatory to entering the field of law. But after studying for only a few weeks he suddenly rejected the whole idea and applied for admission at the town's Augustinian monastery.

Hans Luther was terribly angry and Martin's university friends were astounded. Why had he taken such a step? Many factors contributed, but in the final analysis his decision to become a monk can be summed up in the words "religious experience."

His parents were God-fearing people whose piety undoubtedly had an early influence on him. He shared fear of the horrors of hell, purgatory, and the last judgment which was common to people at the close of the middle ages. In the university library he had found a complete Bible and was tremendously impressed with his own ignorance of its contents. He attended church and daily chapel devotions regularly all through school. His introspective nature made him starkly aware of his sins and shortcomings. Life as a monk was held to be the best way to forgiveness and heaven.

Several grim incidents increased his anxiety. While on a holiday from the university he accidentally severed an artery in his leg with his student sword. He almost bled to death and in distress prayed to the Virgin Mary for help. The death of a number of students during a plague moved him profoundly. While returning to Erfurt, following a visit to Mansfeld, he was caught in a heavy thunderstorm and a bolt of lightning struck so close that he was knocked to the ground. Overcome by panic he invoked St. Anna for aid and vowed "Help me, and I will become a monk." Fifteen days later, on July 17, friends accompanied him to the gate of the "Black Cloister," monastery of the Order of Augustinian Hermits in Erfurt.

That this decision came later in life than usually was the case, and that his impressionable years had been spent not within the confines of a monastery but in the unrestricted atmosphere of a great university, later proved valuable to him and to the Protestant Church.

1.3 Monk and Priest

Luther was not received immediately into the monastery but had to remain for several months in the monastic hostelry examining himself and being examined. In September, 1505, all parties being satisfied, his head was shaved and he was invested with the black Augustinian habit and cowl, and formally received as a novice.

He scrubbed the floors, begged in the streets, and engaged in various ascetic and spiritual exercises. When his probationary year was ended Luther took the vows of obedience, poverty, and chastity and was received into the order of the Augustinian monks. His sincere piety and scholarship so impressed his superiors that he was urged to prepare for the priesthood, and, on April 4, 1507, was ordained to that office.

The petty employments of the monastery did not consume all of Luther's energy and he devoted himself strenuously to studying the scholastic theology available at that time. However, long hours with books did little to ease his mind and give him the peace of conscience he sought within the cloister walls. The books taught him to rely on his own efforts to procure favor with God, and he was too honest to believe that his penitence was deep enough and his fastings worthy enough to compensate for his sins.

Although his heart was not at rest, Luther continued to perform his priestly duties and undertake any new tasks assigned to him. In the fall of 1508 he was appointed to the chair of moral philosophy which had been entrusted to the Augustinians by the faculty at the newly established University of Wittenberg. Desiring to teach theology rather than logic and ethics, he availed himself of this opportunity to study for a bachelor's degree which would permit him to lecture on certain books of the Bible. He had virtually completed his studies when he was called back to Erfurt in October, 1509. There he lectured in the monastery for about a year, and in November, 1510, was sent in company with another monk on a mission to Rome.

In the Holy City he visited as many shrines and churches as possible. His high opinion of the papal court was lowered by his observations of its reckless luxury and scandal, but his confidence in the church remained unshaken.

2

THE PROFESSOR

2.1 Dr. Luther

LUTHER RETURNED TO Erfurt from Rome, and in the summer of 1511 was sent as one of three new professors to Wittenberg. Here he came under the influence of John von Staupitz, vicar of the Augustinian order, who showed warm sympathy and understanding toward the earnest young priest.

As yet Luther had been unable to convince himself of God's love, mercy, and forgiveness. His quest carried him along the path of good works, but he never could feel that he had done enough to save himself. He tried the path of confession but concluded there was more wrong with men than could be cleansed by enumerating a list of particular offenses.

Luther's problems of faith did not mount up through clearly defined stages to a sudden soul-free climax. Rather he passed through a series of crises. Staupitz did much to comfort him in some of these grave periods. He encouraged the zealous monk to trust in the God who loved and sent his Son to redeem man, rather than try to appease God through his own works.

Staupitz' theology was quite different from Luther's. It admitted man's weakness and called him to completely submerge himself in God. There was no striving, no assertion of self. Eventually the individual found peace in a blissful atmosphere surrounded entirely by God. Luther's efforts were virtually the opposite. His every act was replete with self-assertion directed toward winning merit. He tried the mystical way of Staupitz but could never completely lose himself in the essence of a God whom he conceived to be an angry judge.

Luther's troubled spirit did not lower him in the vicar's estimation and, perhaps to get his mind off it, Staupitz advised him to study for a doctor's degree and assume the chair of Bible at the university. It was good medicine, for thus the distressed monk came to closer grips with the source book of his faith. So far, writings about the Bible, rather than the book itself, had been his main diet. He studied for the degree and preached in the monastery's rickety chapel until October 18-19, 1512, when he became Martin Luther, doctor of sacred scripture, professor of Bible at Wittenberg University.

2.2 The Awakening

Since May, 1512, Luther had been subprior and regent in the school connected with the Black Cloister at Wittenberg. In May, 1515, he became district vicar for Thuringia and Meissen, having eleven monasteries under his care. Meanwhile he was discharging his duties as professor in the university.

Frequently the solution to great problems comes quite undramatically as one goes about the daily tasks. Luther's awakening to a God who makes man righteous in order to save him came in such a way. He knew the teaching that the righteous shall be saved by faith. But who, he asked himself, is righteous?

As he studied and taught, and looked after his wards in the monasteries, he gradually discovered he had been misled by the medieval concept that grace could be earned. This, he found, was contrary to the New Testament. Grace can't be earned. God gives it. Man, therefore, does not make himself righteous. It is God who makes man righteous. He makes man righteous as a free gift (grace) so that he can be saved. Out of this came the doctrine of "justification by faith."

At this point Luther still felt that he was in total agreement with the teachings of the Roman Church. In a humble way he believed that he had discovered for himself what always had been— that he had just been slow in catching on. Deeper study, however, made it clear to him that there was a great difference between his own and the theology of the middle ages. He became convinced that man can contribute nothing toward his salvation, but that God, recognizing man's unrighteousness, had redeemed him and restored him through the sacrifice of his Son, Jesus Christ. This indeed was not the work of an implacable judge, but of a loving Father.

Luther now found himself rejecting most of the medieval writers and teachers. He went back to the Bible, to Christ, and the apostles. Convinced of the truth, he no longer was restrained by contradictory views. His beliefs were contrary to many of the teachings of the church, and while he didn't plan it that way they brought him into open revolt. The matter of indulgences opened the battle.

3

COLLISION WITH ROME

3.1 The Question of Indulgences

THE ROMAN CHURCH taught that forgiveness of sins could be secured only through the sacrament of penance. This required contrition of heart, confession to a priest, and satisfaction by good works. Release from the penalty of eternal punishment was guaranteed by the absolution pronounced by the priest. If not enough works of penance were done before death, however, the remainder had to be atoned for in the torments of purgatory for an indefinite period.

Gradually a custom developed which permitted one to purchase indulgences to offset purgatorial punishment. It was at this point that Luther's theology conflicted with the church's practice. Grace was God's gift, but indulgences implied that man can earn grace.

In 1515 the sale of indulgences was being pressed in the archbishopric of Mainz which had been purchased recently by Albert of Brandenburg. Because of the vast revenues the office controlled, it was a profitable investment to become a bishop in those days. Although not old enough to be a bishop, Albert already had procured two other sees before negotiating for the purchase of Mainz. Pope Leo X was willing to overlook these irregularities in exchange for ten thousand ducats which he needed to complete the Church of St. Peter in Rome.

Albert borrowed the money from the Fuggers banking concern in Augsburg. Then the pope granted him the privilege of selling indulgences so that he could settle his account at the bank and at the same time raise additional sums for St. Peter's.

John Tetzel, a Dominican prior who had displayed shrewd aptitude in selling indulgences, conducted the campaign. He didn't enter Luther's parish because Frederick the Wise, elector of Saxony, had an indulgence traffic of his own in the form of a large collection of relics gathered for veneration in the Castle Church, Wittenberg. However, some of Luther's people crossed the border and bought indulgences from Tetzel. Luther saw the fundamental danger of the traffic when these folk countered his preaching on repentance of heart and life by showing him indulgences remitting their sins. On October 31 Luther tacked a placard on the door of the Castle Church. The sound of his hammer reached to Rome.

3.2 The Ninety-Five Theses

The theses which Luther posted on the church door were not a declaration of revolt. They were, after the custom of the day, an invitation to theologians of Wittenberg and vicinity to debate on the indulgence situation. So that all participants could be prepared, he posted the ninety-five propositions he intended to defend in the debate.

The points for argument did not call for abandonment of indulgences but merely advocated the elimination of evils in the system. Luther maintained, in his theses, that repentance should be a lifelong experience and should manifest itself in a continuing effort to overcome sinful desires. Indulgences, he said, are simply remissions of penalties which the church has imposed. They have no effect on the souls of the departed and they don't remit sin; only God can do that.

Luther believed he was being a loyal defender of the Roman Church by attempting to correct these abuses, and correspondence revealed that he thought the pope was unaware of what was going on. To his surprise the theses released a great flood of favorable public opinion and were applauded as a courageous and unrelenting attack. Within two weeks they were distributed in German as well as Latin throughout Germany.

There had been a growing dislike of the indulgence system and of the pope's interference in what, to the Germans, were strictly their own national affairs. The theses now became a rallying point not only for those who opposed Rome's continuous exploitation of German finances but also for those who resented the dominating attitude of a foreign power. Even though they attacked one of his own pet institutions, the Elector Frederick stood by his daring young monk.

As the Augustinians rallied around Luther, the Dominicans upheld the cause of Brother Tetzel. He was granted a doctor's degree largely to enable him to publish some theses of his own.

When the Tetzel writings came off press and were distributed, students at Wittenberg collected a large quantity and held a public bonfire. Luther, still a loyal son of the monastic system, was greatly displeased by their sophomoric act.

3.3 Rome Moves to Attack

Luther sent a copy of his theses to Albert of Brandenburg who forwarded them to Rome where Pope Leo X reportedly brushed the incident off as a row between rival monastic orders. Later the Dominicans charged Luther with heresy and formal proceedings were begun. On August 7, 1518, Luther received notice to appear in Rome for trial within sixty days.

By no means a coward, Luther was nonetheless unwilling to be the victim of a mock-trial in the territory of the enemy. He asked Elector Frederick to have the trial transferred to German soil where he might at least have the benefit of impartial judges.

On second thought the pope decided not to wait sixty days and ordered the elector to arrest Luther at once and turn him over to Cardinal Cajetan for delivery in Rome. Although Frederick was not sympathetic to heresy he was determined that the man who had brought so much attention to his university at Wittenberg should have fair play. He prevailed upon the pope to have Cardinal Cajetan give Luther a personal hearing in Augsburg where he would be attending a diet or parliament.

In a benign manner the cardinal offered to help Luther out of all his difficulty if he would simply submit to the pope's authority and retract his errors. Luther of course refused and tried to defend his positions. A fruitless and oft-times heated controversy ensued and at the end of three days Cajetan told Luther to leave his presence and not return until he was ready to recant.

The cardinal was quite upset by the Augsburg incident and wrote Elector Frederick a letter calling upon him to turn the heretical monk over to the Roman authorities. Frederick's reply indicated his increasing resistance to papal dictatorship. He asked for a free trial and a statement of Luther's errors in writing.

The pope's chamberlain, Carl von Miltitz, was dispatched to Germany in an attempt to rectify Cajetan's blundering. He correctly estimated that much of the populace was on Luther's side and the time for forcibly suppressing him was past. Resorting to diplomacy he persuaded Luther to have his case submitted to a German bishop and to refrain from further attack in the meantime. Luther agreed, but only on the condition that his opponents would remain silent too.

4

THE BREACH
WIDENS

4.1 Pushed into the Arena

EVEN WHILE LUTHER was meeting with Miltitz circumstances were shaping up which drove him to break silence. He had stated his willingness to recant if someone proved his error. An ambitious professor at the University of Ingolstadt, John Eck, with an enviable reputation as a disputant, saw in this his opportunity to win renown and also favor with Rome.

Andrew Carlstadt of the Wittenberg faculty had espoused the cause of Luther publicly and had been engaged in an extended debate with Eck through the medium of pamphlets. Now a public debate between the two was arranged for Leipzig. In preparation Eck drew up a series of twelve theses, directed not so much at his differences with Carlstadt as with the theology of Luther.

The champion of Roman orthodoxy clearly was baiting Luther into the arena.

After months of wrangling about procedures and proper invitations, and with much pomp and pageantry, the debate got under way on June 27, 1519. Several hundred Wittenberg students were there—a sixteenth-century sort of college cheering section. During the ensuing eighteen days of debate they frequently became embroiled with the Leipzig University students who sided with Eck. Carlstadt and Eck matched wits for four days over the relation between grace and free will. The erudition and cleverness of Eck gave him a decided advantage over the Wittenberg scholar, but spectator interest was being reserved for July 4 when Luther would take the field.

For another four days Eck and Luther discussed the divine right of the pope with the Ingolstadter insisting that the divine plan of government was a monarchy with the pope at its head. Luther agreed that the church was a monarchy but that Christ was its head. The passage in St. Matthew concerning the rock upon which Christ would build his church was quoted by Eck with the interpretation that Peter was the "rock" and since he also was the first pope it was clear that papal supremacy had been established by Christ.

Luther declared the passage should be considered along with Peter's previous statement, "Thou art the Christ...." This confession, he said, is the "rock" on which Christ built his church.

4.2 The Shadow of Hus

The crisis at Leipzig was reached when Eck backed into a dialectical corner and had to resort to foul tactics. How discredit Luther? Perhaps if he made him synonymous with heresy....

Craftily Eck pointed out the similarity between Luther's arguments and those of the Bohemian reformer, John Hus, whom the Council of Constance had condemned to the stake a century before. Luther denounced the insinuation and declared the Bohemian heresy irrelevant to the debate.

It was inevitable in opposing the Roman Church's contention to primacy that Luther would use arguments similar to those of previous reformers. The condemnation of Hus as a heretic did not necessarily make all of his views heretical. In fact, Luther insisted, some of Hus's articles were genuinely Christian and evangelical.

The spectators and visiting theologians were stunned, and perhaps Luther shocked even himself. Clearly his remark would be interpreted to mean that the general councils—the highest earthly authority—were not beyond fault. This was heresy.

Luther had long been aware of the need for reform in the church. As his ideas developed it became apparent that the pope was not above human weakness. The church militant needed an earthly head, and for the sake of good order it was necessary that he be obeyed. But that didn't make him infallible. After all, he was human.

Now this same reasoning had pushed from Luther's lips the admission that councils could err also. Unwittingly Eck had contributed what probably was the greatest outcome of the debate—Luther's growing conviction that even general councils could be unreliable. Henceforth he would take his stand on the unassailable Word of God as revealed in the Scriptures.

Results of the debate were weighed by judges at the University of Paris who condemned Luther and his views as heretical. When Philip Melanchthon, a Wittenberg associate and close friend of Luther, questioned the opinion on the basis of Scripture, the Parisians looked down their noses at the upstart, informing him they were chief among the few to whom interpretation of Scripture could be entrusted.

4.3 For Such a Time as This

Luther was frankly disappointed with the outcome of the debate. He had hoped his opinions would be accepted and reformation of the church effected.

The controversy did much, however, to crystallize his own views: The pope did not have absolute authority; a council can err in its decisions; the Bible is above popes and councils in authority; the Church of Christ is not limited to the Roman fellowship alone but is the community of believers throughout the world.

Gradually Luther realized these views differed so fundamentally from those of Rome that there was small chance of healing the breach. The notion that he might become a martyr recurred frequently but it didn't cause him to relinquish his zeal. In fact he received inspiration from it and kept three presses rolling at full speed to turn out tracts, sermons, and commentaries.

In addition to the Leipzig debate, the summer of 1519 brought forth another event which was significant in Luther's life. Maximilian, the Holy Roman Emperor, died in January and the election of a successor was of utmost concern to the rulers and populace of Europe. Consequently, there was rejoicing in Germany on June 28 when the electors named Charles of Spain in preference to Francis of France. Charles was a Hapsburg and the Germans confidently expected he would unite them into a strong, independent nation. However, the new emperor favored his Spanish mother more than his German father and treated his fatherland like an outlying province of Spain.

Wide distribution of the Ninety-five Theses and other writings, as well as prominence resulting from the Leipzig encounter, had fixed the eyes of many Germans upon Luther. When Charles failed to step into the role of national figure they switched their enthusiasm to Luther. Few understood his ideas on Christianity but they believed he could lead them to political, intellectual, and economic freedom. Scholars, princes, knights, and commoners gathered about the Wittenberg professor who had demonstrated his fearlessness in the face of tyranny. Gradually Luther sensed his mission as leader in a mighty movement. History called it the Reformation.

5

LUTHER EXPLAINS HIMSELF

5.1 The Christian Nobility

LUTHER'S ATTEMPTS TO interest the pope in reform had proved futile. He was likewise unsuccessful in having a general council convened to consider his propositions. Now, in the first of three great treatises, he called upon the secular rulers to concern themselves with the state of the church.

Appearing in August, 1520, the "Open Letter to the Christian Nobility of the German Nation" flatly attacked corruption among the clergy and prodded the laity into doing something about it. Since all Christians are priests before God, Luther held it was incumbent upon them and particularly upon Christian rulers to feel responsible for the conduct of the church within their domains. As Christians they should abhor vice and wickedness regardless of whether it flourished on the main street or in the monastery.

No one, said the open letter, has been able to reform the Romanists because they have erected three walls of defense, "*First*, when pressed by the temporal power, they have made decrees and said that the temporal power has no jurisdiction over them. *Second*, when the attempt is made to reprove them out of the Scriptures, they raise the objection that the interpretation of the Scriptures belongs to no one except the pope. *Third*, if threatened with a council, they answer with the fable that no one can call a council but the pope."

Luther demolished the first wall by showing that everyone is equal before God. Those holding the title of priest or bishop are not superior to other Christians nor do they differ except in vocation, by which also a cobbler differs from a blacksmith. The title of "priest" is conferred by laymen who themselves are priests in the sight of God. Thus the holder of a church title is not beyond the reach of temporal government.

He breached the second wall by pointing out that every enlightened Christian—layman or priest—has the right to seek God's message for him in the Scriptures. The third wall tumbled through Luther's insistence that every man, as a priest, shares responsibility for right management in the church.

5.2 The Babylonian Captivity

Before his letter to the nobility was off press, Luther was writing his second treatise, "The Babylonian Captivity of the Church." The first had been primarily for lay people while the second was for theologians. It aimed directly at freeing the Christian fellowship in Europe from the "captivity" of the Roman sacramental system.

The Roman Church taught that it alone could dispense the saving grace associated with the sacraments, and that the sacramental acts could be performed only by ordained priests. Anyone who denied that the church controlled the flow of grace from God was striking Catholicism in its most vital spot. Without its sacramental system Rome could no longer bind its subjects. This was the front at which Luther aimed his heaviest artillery.

He reiterated his views on the priesthood of believers. Priests should be servants of the people who comprise the church, rather than servants of a papal hierarchy. They cannot interfere with grace. It is God's free gift to the individual believer.

In the course of his treatise Luther also asserted that there are only two sacraments—baptism and the Lord's Supper—rather than seven as taught in Roman Catholicism. A sacrament, he held, had to be instituted by Christ, contain a divine promise of the forgiveness of sins, and make use of an earthly element (water, bread, wine). Confirmation, ordination, marriage, penance, and extreme unction were rejected as sacraments because they lacked some of the prescribed characteristics.

The mass had been seen as a repetition of Christ's incarnation and crucifixion at the hands of a priest before the altar. By this sacrifice man tried to earn grace. Now it became the Lord's Supper—a communion of the believing Christian with his Saviour. Both the bread and the wine should be received by the communicant, Luther insisted. While Christ is really present in the elements, the bread does not become flesh nor the wine blood through a magical act called transubstantiation. Moreover, Christ is not sacrificed anew whenever the mass is celebrated. His sacrifice on the cross was for all time. Through that sacrifice a man's sins are remitted if he has faith.

5.3 Christian Liberty

Miltitz, the papal nuncio who previously had failed to reconcile Luther and the pope, tried again in October, 1520. He had Luther agree to write a letter to Leo X assuring him that there was nothing personal in his attacks on the papacy.

In the letter, Luther cautioned Leo against listening to those of his advisers who would make him a demigod, who put him above councils, who make him the final authority in interpreting Scripture, "for through them Satan already has made much headway." He also assured Leo that he was an obedient servant of the church and that he was not inveighing against him personally.

Accompanying the letter was a copy of Luther's latest pamphlet, "A Treatise on Christian Liberty." It expresses calm Christian reflection quite different from the theological conflicts which were carried forward in his other treatises. At the outset it poses two propositions which seem to be a paradox: "A Christian man is a perfectly free lord of all, subject to none," and "A Christian man is a perfectly dutiful servant of all, subject to all."

The first proposition acknowledges man as a sinner, but one who has been liberated and restored to a right relationship with God through justifying grace. In justifying man, God has freed him from the consequence of his sins because of Christ's atonement.

This freedom affects a man's whole life. Not only is he free from the consequences of sin, but he is no longer shackled by his own hates, passions, and wilful desires. Because this freedom is based on his own personal relationship with God, no one can interfere. He is "subject to none."

The second proposition indicates that the free man's life takes a different direction. Originally he was concerned with himself, but now the reborn person, in gratitude for his own freedom, serves his neighbor. His motive is not merely humanitarian, but stems out of a sincere desire to help others become free too. Love permits him to do no less than become the servant of all.

The treatise and letter would have scant effect on Pope Leo. Five months previously he had signed a bull excommunicating Luther.

5.4 The Papal Bull

A chronological listing of events can be misleading—for instance those concerning the papal bull. It was signed by Leo on June 15, 1520. It reached Luther officially on October 10. He immediately wrote a fiery epistle denouncing it and Eck, whose style and invective he recognized. Aware that the bull was being circulated and that his literature was being burned, he nevertheless sat down in November and wrote a friendly letter to the pope accompanying it with his treatise on Christian liberty.

On the surface this would indicate insincerity, but events shaped up to prove he was being consistent. Although he knew he had personal enemies, he never lost sight of the fact that he was fighting a system rather than individuals. The pope, for him, was merely a figurehead, in this instance the symbol of an intolerable autocracy in an area where individual freedom before God was essential.

The papal bull credited Luther with forty-one errors, called for the burning of his books, charged heresy, gave him sixty days to submit, and warned everyone against sheltering him in his excommunication. Distribution of the bull was in the hands of Eck and papal legate Jerome Aleander. They succeeded in posting copies of the bull and burning books in several cities, but largely their efforts were unsuccessful due to strenuous opposition by the German people.

On December 10, probably in reprisal for a book-burning at Cologne, Melanchthon posted a notice on the Wittenberg University bulletin board inviting students and faculty to a bonfire outside the Elster gate of the city. Books on scholastic theology, and especially those works of canon law on which the pope and the Roman hierarchy based their claims to power, were tossed into the flames. Then Luther stepped forward quietly and with a prayer on his lips added the booklet containing the papal bull to the fire. He and the professors withdrew but the students made a holiday of the affair, parading and singing throughout the town and burning books of Luther's opponents.

Significantly, the bonfire marked the end of the sixty-day period of grace. From now on no one was to communicate with Luther or provide him with the necessities of life. In the eyes of Rome he was an outlaw.

6

THE MONK
STANDS FIRM

6.1 The Diet of Worms

OVERTONES OF INTRIGUE and statecraft are
dominant in the prelude to the imperial assembly at Worms. The church at Rome had given its
decision. Would the secular authorities now take
action and turn him over to the papal authorities?

Charles, at his coronation as emperor, had
subscribed to the imperial constitution which said
no German should be taken outside his country
for trial, and also that no one should be outlawed
without a hearing. Frederick the Wise, Luther's
elector, took no action against him, using these
same reasons as an excuse. Aleander, the papal
representative, wanted the case settled arbitrarily
by the emperor since he was well aware of the support Luther would receive at a public hearing.
The man had been condemned by the church, he

argued, and as good churchmen the rulers should simply apprehend the Wittenberg monk without a further examination of his views.

For the first three months of 1521 the diet devoted itself chiefly to transacting state business. During this period Emperor Charles changed his mind several times about inviting the Wittenberg monk for a hearing. Finally, on March 6, against his will, he offered Luther a safe-conduct to Worms.

In a two-wheeled cart Luther and a few companions set out from Wittenberg on April 2. Cities along the way welcomed him and invited him to preach, but no reception equaled the one on his arrival at Worms. When the party was sighted from the cathedral tower at 10 A. M., on April 16, a group of horsemen dashed out to act as an escort through the city gate. Two thousand spectators thronged the streets so that Luther was barely able to reach his lodging in the house of the Knights of St. John.

He was summoned to appear at four o'clock the following afternoon, and because of the crowds in the streets was conducted through gardens and alleys to the episcopal palace where the diet was meeting. When the door of the assembly hall was opened, Luther was ushered through a company of princes, nobles, and ecclesiastics to the foot of a canopied chair. On it sat Charles, the twenty-one-year-old emperor. Near by was a table loaded with books.

6.2 Answer Without Horns

After the opening courtesies had been dispatched the presiding officer, an official of the archbishop of Trier, pointed to the books, asked Luther if he was the author, and if he was ready to retract what he had written.

Luther had been instructed to speak only in answer to direct questions and was not to seek a discussion. However, this double question could not be answered yes or no. He paused and his legal adviser asked that the titles be read. Luther then acknowledged that the books were his.

Again the question, "Will you retract...?"

The monk believed his writing was an accurate interpretation of God's Word. In his mind was Christ's admonition to the disciples "whosoever shall deny me before men, him will I also deny before my Father...." Since salvation was involved he asked time to think over the answer. The diet agreed that he should return at four the next afternoon.

After a night of prayer Luther again appeared before the impressive assembly. This time a larger hall had been chosen because of the tremendous crowd. Again the formalities, and again the question, but this time phrased a bit differently. "Do you defend all of your books or are you willing to recall some things?" This was the opening Luther had been seeking and he quickly shaped his strategy to take advantage of it. They were forcing him to make a speech since a categorical answer was impossible.

The books were in three classes, Luther explained. The first was purely devotional and had been commended even by his enemies. The second was against the papacy. If he recanted these he would open the door to further tyranny and impiety. The third class inveighed against individuals, and in these he admitted he had used caustic and intemperate language. Still the facts had to stand unless refuted by the Scriptures, in which case he would be first to cast his books into the fires.

Obviously the diet could not at this moment disprove his works by the Bible. There was a consultation. The interrogator turned to Luther. "Give us a direct answer—one without horns. Will you or will you not recant your errors?"

6.3 Neither Right nor Safe

The Spanish guards were mentally stacking faggots around the lonely little figure in the middle of the room. Princes, nobles, and the Holy Roman Emperor leaned forward to catch his words.

"Since Your Majesty and Your Lordships want a direct reply, I will answer without horns or teeth," he began quietly.

The spectators looked at each other significantly, then back to the earnest friar. Confidence was returning and his voice carried plainly to all corners of the room.

"Unless convinced by the testimony of Scripture or right reason—for I trust neither the pope nor councils inasmuch as they have often erred and contradicted one another—I am bound in conscience, held captive by the Word of God in the Scriptures I have quoted. I neither can nor will recant anything, for it is neither right nor safe to act against conscience. God help me! Amen."

There was silence for an instant. Then pandemonium broke loose. The interrogator tried to restore order but the emperor walked out and the meeting adjourned. Luther was escorted back to his rooms by the admiring populace. Nobles who had been on the fringe now openly praised the courageous preacher and vowed their support. During the night warning notices were surreptitiously posted on the doors of his enemies.

Charles summoned the electors and princes the following day to decide what should be done. His own impulse to condemn Luther right away was restrained because he needed the good will of the Germans in other measures coming before the diet. A plan was evolved whereby a select group of theologians would call on Luther and try to effect a reconciliation through persuasion. The discussion always bogged down when Luther insisted he must be persuaded on the basis of Scripture.

Having received a twenty-one-day safe-conduct Luther set out for Wittenberg on April 26. The diet closed officially on May 25, and the next day, following a rump session of prejudiced nobles, the emperor signed the Edict of Worms. According to it, Luther was the devil himself in a monk's habit. He was to be seized on sight and turned over to the emperor—an outlaw of the church and the state.

7

DRASTIC CHANGES

7.1 Wartburg to Wittenberg

Fortunately for Luther there was more than noisy adulation among the people. A few sober minds knew how relentless the papal wolves would be in tracking him down after the safe-conduct expired, and so a "kidnapping" and removal to a safe place was planned.

Luther made a detour along the road to Wittenberg in order to visit relatives at Möhra. For months the outside world knew only that he had been captured near there in the Thuringian forest by a band of knights. Many lamented him as dead, but gradually the flow of thorny letters to his adversaries and the new treatises rolling from the press allayed their fears.

By a circuitous route Luther had been conveyed to the Wartburg, an ancient fortress-castle near Eisenach. He arrived on May 4 and, with the exception of short trips into the forest and to near-by villages, did not leave for seven months. To outward appearances he was Junker George, a carefree, bearded knight with sword swinging impressively at his side. The secret was well kept and at the outset even the elector, who authorized the masquerade, did not know Luther's whereabouts.

Luther chafed at his forced inactivity, and, ever the monk, fell to contemplation and examination of himself. Could past generations and earlier scholars have been so completely out of step with the gospel? Could a mere friar be right against them all? Might he not be in error and drag many others to eternal damnation?

Hard work helped take his mind off his problems. During his stay in the Wartburg, in addition to correspondence and pamphlets, he authored a work on confession, expositions on several Psalms, a commentary on the Magnificat, had a volume of sermons on the Epistles and Gospels well underway, and had translated the entire New Testament into German.

Prayer and study restored his conviction. To doubt, or even to remain silent was like going against conscience—neither right nor safe. With conviction came a sense of divine commission. When events called him back into the world again he went courageously and with determination. He was a revolutionary, but a conservative one. That quality is what took him back to Wittenberg.

7.2 From Freedom to License

So often a new movement suffers from overenthusiasm. The Reformation was no exception in this respect. Zealots took the usual shortcut from bondage to freedom by way of turmoil instead of restrained orderly procedure.

In parts of Germany the old ways were thrown off hastily. Organs, paintings, and statues were thrown from the churches, vestments were discarded, bread and wine were both administered to the laity, priests married, nuns took husbands, monastic vows were renounced, various forms of the mass were discontinued, priests and worshipers who persisted in the traditional forms were attacked.

Rumors of violent acts reached the Wartburg. Luther, still in the guise of Junker George, made a hurried trip to Wittenberg early in December, 1521. Matters there had not yet reached the unrestrained stage which they later assumed. Nevertheless he cautioned the people in a "warning against riot and rebellion," written on his return to the Wartburg.

In it he reasoned that reform is not so much a matter of externals as of faith. Breaking up the furniture in a church does not change the heart of a man. Vandalism is by no means a sign of repentance and trust in God—in fact it approaches the old form of seeking favor through works. Giving wine as well as bread in the Lord's Supper is not as important as the spiritual attitude of the communicant.

Finally the tumult in Wittenberg reached the point where he had to step in, so—in the face of the imperial ban—he returned on March 6, 1522. Insisting that no drastic change should be made until, through re-education, those affected requested it as a matter of faith, he restored order in the university city in a remarkably short time.

The peasants meanwhile took the shortcut to freedom, too, in a series of bloody uprisings. Chafing under their bondage to the nobles, they adapted Luther's "free lord of all" statement to their own demands for social reform. Luther preached the Christian duty of submission to lawful authority, but the peasants ravaged and plundered until finally defeated in 1525. It was a dark hour in the Reformation.

7.3 Pigtails on the Pillow

WITTENBERG, June 14—Katherine von Bora, 26, late of the Cistercian nunnery at Nimbschen, and Martin Luther, 42, professor of Bible at the local university, were married last night at a simple ceremony in the Black Cloister. Dr. John Bugenhagen officiated. In attendance were Artist Lucas Cranach and Mrs. Cranach; Dr. Justus Jonas, prior of Castle Church; and John Apel, professor of law at the university....

If there had been newspapers in 1525, Luther's wedding might have been announced to the public in this way. However, newspapers weren't to appear until much later, and the lack of publicity gave gossips and slanderers choice opportunity to vilify the former monk and nun. The malicious stories were partly offset by a public ceremony, complete with a special service in the town church, a wedding dinner in the cloister, and a dance at the town hall on June 27.

The wedding was a direct result of Luther's reform teachings. He disliked the monastic system because men and women sought merit before God through restraints and vows rather than depending upon grace. Celibacy, he had written earlier, is not founded on Scripture but marriage is. These teachings found their way into many cloisters and convents, among them the one at Nimbschen where Katherine von Bora, at the age of sixteen, had been received into the Cistercian Order.

She and eleven other nuns sought Luther's assistance in effecting a plan of escape. Although he had no idea of what it would involve for him personally, he arranged for them to be smuggled out of the convent in empty fish barrels on the day before Easter in 1523. The plan succeeded and some of the nuns came to Wittenberg where they found homes, husbands, or new positions. Two years later Kathie was the only one not permanently cared for despite Luther's several attempts at matchmaking. Then the spunky miss hinted rather boldly that the Reformer himself would be an acceptable husband and he resolved to take the course which he had urged on so many others.

It was strange for one accustomed to solitude. "Formerly at the table I was alone," he wrote, "now I am with someone. When I awaken I see a pair of pigtails on the pillow which were not there before."

7.4 The Cloister Becomes a Home

Marriage probably extended Luther's life for a number of years. Previously he and his dog enjoyed an irregular sort of existence in the Black Cloister. Dishes were covered with dust, the bed hadn't been made in over a year, his clothes were in disorder. Sometimes Luther forgot his meals altogether and at other times stuffed himself.

The vigor with which his industrious wife established order can be imagined by his reference to her as "my lord Kathie." She was an efficient housekeeper and thrifty manager of what little they possessed at the outset. Neither had any money. Luther refused pay for his writing, although the publishers grew rich, nor did he receive any tax revenues from the cloister since he had laid aside his cowl.

Things improved when the elector gave Luther the cloister for a home, and adjacent to it a vegetable garden with a small brew house where Kathie prepared the family beverage. His small salary as professor was augmented somewhat when they took in boarding students attending the university.

The Luthers had six children. Two of them died in childhood, but otherwise the family enjoyed a merry, wholesome life. The house was always full of visitors—some of them more or less permanent—including traveling dignitaries, numerous aunts and relatives, monks and nuns seeking a permanent residence, and four orphaned children from among their kinsfolk. Because it was large and suitable, the cloister sometimes was used as a hospital, and it was not unusual for the "family" to number as many as twenty-five. Guests who stayed for any length of time were expected to take part in household duties, participate in daily prayers, catechetical study, and family devotions. Music, singing, chess, and outdoor bowling were forms of recreation. Through Kathie's economy, improvements were made in the Luther house. An orchard, hop garden, and finally a farm were purchased.

When Luther worried about his children's future he overcame it with faith. A pious training is most important, he wrote. It is good to leave an inheritance, but preparing children to manage wisely is more important. We parents are fools if we don't train them to fear God, to control themselves, and to live honorably.

8

A CHURCH REBORN

8.1 The National Conscience

THE PEOPLE AT WITTENBERG and in other cities of influence were gradually learning to think of the church as separate from the Roman hierarchy. Now there was need for reorganization. A steady supply of ministers was essential and arrangements had to be made for their training and support. A bond of some sort was necessary to establish unity of endeavor, and mission work was imperative in areas where conviction had lapsed into indifference.

Luther didn't care for organizational work. The thought that the new church might degenerate into a system of laws and regulations haunted him. Although his revised order of worship was finding its way into use he felt that still more urgent matters demanded attention. Proper instruction of young and old was essential and to accomplish it there had to be some sort of oversight.

The bishops had neglected instruction of the laymen and the princes were loath to reinstitute it. Luther, therefore, laid the task directly upon the congregations and in some cases the city councils to select competent men as pastors, establish pastoral districts, and set up schools. To advise and assist in this work, visitation committees comprising learned laymen and theologians traveled throughout Saxony beginning in 1527. The visitation was carried on in other areas of Germany too, and in this way the groundwork for future organization began.

In the meantime two distinct factions had developed among the princes of Germany. One espoused the Roman cause, the other the Reformation. From 1525 to 1529 a series of diets and assemblies was held. The rival princes concerned themselves largely with attempts at, and opposition to, the invoking of the ban against Luther, his works, and his cohorts which had been executed at Worms. At Speyer in 1529 the Catholic princes, with the emperor's backing, tried to force a resolution preventing the spread of Luther's teachings in any new areas, but the Reformation princes protested. Matters concerning salvation were of an individual nature and could not be legislated. Conscience bound them to oppose the resolution. Principles which the Wittenberg monk had declared only eight years before were becoming the national mind.

8.2 The Augsburg Confession

Sparks of the Reformation had caught fire elsewhere in Europe developing into Reformed, Mennonite, Anabaptist, and other denominations. A major purpose of the diet called by Emperor Charles at Augsburg in 1530 was to harmonize these various groups and attempt a final reconciliation with Rome. To this end each body was to define its teaching in a statement or confession, but not all were represented at the diet and only three were actually submitted.

As usual the papists were laying for the Lutherans. They had prejudiced the emperor against a fair hearing and were reserving their best ammunition for the Saxon "heretics," fully confident that a Lutheran defeat would speedily bring the downfall of the others.

Still under imperial ban, Luther could not attend the diet but stayed at a castle in Coburg from which he advised Melanchthon and others appearing before the emperor. The confession, a series of twenty-eight articles setting forth the Lutheran position, was read on June 25. The first twenty-one present fundamental doctrines of the Scriptures regarding God, Original Sin, the Son of God, Justification, the Church, the Sacraments, Civil Affairs, the Freedom of Will, the Cause of Sin, Good Works, and the Worship of Saints; while the last seven treat of Roman abuses which contradict the Word of God.

The emperor commissioned the Roman theologians to prepare a refutation. On the basis of it he rejected the Lutheran confession, ordered church property restored to Roman bishops, and forbade witnessing and the printing or sale of Lutheran writings.

Dejected by their failure to reform the church, the Lutherans went home in the fall of 1530 unaware that their confession would become a basic creed of the largest Protestant body in the world.

Threatened with coercion by the Romanists in Germany, they joined with other Protestants in 1531 to form the League of Schmalkalden. War was averted when the emperor enlisted both groups to meet the Turkish invasion of Austria, and armed conflict over religious principles was delayed until the summer of 1546. Luther didn't see it. A few months earlier he went to stand before the Judge he had learned to love instead of fear.

8.3 Back to Eisleben

The circuit of Luther's life was completed in Eisleben, his birthplace, where he had gone to mediate between the princes of Mansfeld. He died early on the morning of February 18, 1546, after fervently committing himself to God's keeping and reaffirming the doctrines he had preached.

Luther's lifetime was marked with concern—concern first about himself and God. It wasn't selfish; a man has to find his treasure before he can share it. Luther had searched through lonely tormented hours in a monastery; he brushed aside centuries of proud speculation until he found the truth. It was written in a book, the record of God's revelation of himself to man—the Bible. From it he learned that God is love instead of wrath; that no one, pope or king, can stand between man and that love, or gain it for another; that one can't even win it for himself. It is God's free gift.

Then his concern was for others. This treasure was too priceless to keep; he had to give it away. He preached it, though all the forces of evil railed against him. He printed it, though emperors ordered him to stop the press. He sang it and helped the church to sing—in tones so soft they lull a child to sleep; in battlecries resounding from the ramparts of his mighty-fortress God.

"The devil prefers blockheads," he said, therefore, "the school must be the next thing to the church." Concern led him to teach. Professor was the only job he held—but that for all his life. He hated those who arrogantly claimed sole right to knowledge. So that each might know the truth himself, and in that truth be free, he translated the sacred Scriptures. Matthew to Revelation first, and then the Old Testament were translated, not in high-sounding phrase or platitude, but in majestic simplicity—the words of Hans and Hilda. The lords and ladies would understand it that way too.

The principles of faith which Luther proclaimed, brought fame and the promise of power. But the words addressed to the nobles at Worms recount the humility of his service: "I seek nothing beyond reforming the church in conformity with the Scriptures. I reserve nothing but to bear witness to the Word of God alone."

9

CHRONOLOGY

1483	November 10	Martin Luther born at Eisleben
1484		Family moves to Mansfeld
1497		Luther goes to Magdeburg school
1498		Luther goes to Eisenach school
1501		Enters University of Erfurt
1505		Receives master of arts degree
	July 2	Vows to become a monk
	July 17	Enters Augustinian cloister at Erfurt
1507	April 4	Ordained to priesthood
1508		Teaches at Wittenberg
1509		Lectures at University of Erfurt
1510	November	Begins journey to Rome

1511		Returns to Wittenberg as professor
1512	October 18-19	Receives doctor of sacred scripture degree
1517	October 31	Posts ninety-five theses
1518	August	Pope wants Luther brought to Rome
1519	July 4-14	Luther debates with Eck at Leipzig
1520	June 15	Papal bull signed
	October 10	Luther receives bull
	December 10	Luther burns bull
1521	January 27	Diet of Worms begins
	April 16	Arrives at Worms
	April 17	Makes first statement
	April 18	Luther will not recant
	April 26	Leaves Worms
	May 4	Arrives at the Wartburg
	May 26	Banned by Edict of Worms
1522	March 6	Returns to Wittenberg
1525	June 13	Marries Katherine von Bora
1527		Composition of "A Mighty Fortress"
1530	June 25	Augsburg Confession read
1534		Publishes complete Bible in German
1546	February 18	Luther dies at Eisleben

10

THE 95 THESES

*Disputation of Doctor Martin Luther on the
Power and Efficacy of Indulgences*

OCTOBER 31, 1517

Out of love for the truth and the desire to bring
it to light, the following propositions will be
discussed at Wittenberg, under the presidency
of the Reverend Father Martin Luther, Master
of Arts and of Sacred Theology, and Lecturer in
Ordinary on the same at that place. Wherefore
he requests that those who are unable to be present and debate orally with us, may do so by letter.

In the Name our Lord Jesus Christ. Amen.

1. Our Lord and Master Jesus Christ, when
   He said *Poenitentiam agite*, willed that
   the whole life of believers should be repentance.

2. This word cannot be understood to mean sacramental penance, i.e., confession and satisfaction, which is administered by the priests.

3. Yet it means not inward repentance only; nay, there is no inward repentance which does not outwardly work divers mortifications of the flesh.

4. The penalty [of sin], therefore, continues so long as hatred of self continues; for this is the true inward repentance, and continues until our entrance into the kingdom of heaven.

5. The pope does not intend to remit, and cannot remit any penalties other than those which he has imposed either by his own authority or by that of the Canons.

6. The pope cannot remit any guilt, except by declaring that it has been remitted by God and by assenting to God's remission; though, to be sure, he may grant remission in cases reserved to his judgment. If his right to grant remission in such cases were despised, the guilt would remain entirely unforgiven.

7. God remits guilt to no one whom He does not, at the same time, humble in all things and bring into subjection to His vicar, the priest.

8. The penitential canons are imposed only on the living, and, according to them, nothing should be imposed on the dying.

9. Therefore the Holy Spirit in the pope is kind to us, because in his decrees he always makes exception of the article of death and of necessity.

10. Ignorant and wicked are the doings of those priests who, in the case of the dying, reserve canonical penances for purgatory.

11. This changing of the canonical penalty to the penalty of purgatory is quite evidently one of the tares that were sown while the bishops slept.

12. In former times the canonical penalties were imposed not after, but before absolution, as tests of true contrition.

13. The dying are freed by death from all penalties; they are already dead to canonical rules, and have a right to be released from them.

14. The imperfect health [of soul], that is to say, the imperfect love, of the dying brings with it, of necessity, great fear; and the smaller the love, the greater is the fear.

15. This fear and horror is sufficient of itself alone (to say nothing of other things) to constitute the penalty of purgatory, since it is very near to the horror of despair.

16. Hell, purgatory, and heaven seem to differ as do despair, almost-despair, and the assurance of safety.

17. With souls in purgatory it seems necessary that horror should grow less and love increase.

18. It seems unproved, either by reason or Scripture, that they are outside the state of merit, that is to say, of increasing love.

19. Again, it seems unproved that they, or at least that all of them, are certain or assured of their own blessedness, though we may be quite certain of it.

20. Therefore by "full remission of all penalties" the pope means not actually "of all," but only of those imposed by himself.

21. Therefore those preachers of indulgences are in error, who say that by the pope's indulgences a man is freed from every penalty, and saved;

22. Whereas he remits to souls in purgatory no penalty which, according to the canons, they would have had to pay in this life.

23. If it is at all possible to grant to any one the remission of all penalties whatsoever, it is certain that this remission can be granted only to the most perfect, that is, to the very fewest.

24. It must needs be, therefore, that the greater part of the people are deceived by that indiscriminate and highsounding promise of release from penalty.

25. The power which the pope has, in a general way, over purgatory, is just like the power which any bishop or curate has, in a special way, within his own diocese or parish.

26. The pope does well when he grants remission to souls [in purgatory], not by the power of the keys (which he does not possess), but by way of intercession.

27. They preach man who say that so soon as the penny jingles into the money-box, the soul flies out [of purgatory].

28. It is certain that when the penny jingles into the money-box, gain and avarice can be increased, but the result of the intercession of the Church is in the power of God alone.

29. Who knows whether all the souls in purgatory wish to be bought out of it, as in the legend of Sts. Severinus and Paschal.

30. No one is sure that his own contrition is sincere; much less that he has attained full remission.

31. Rare as is the man that is truly penitent, so rare is also the man who truly buys indulgences, i.e., such men are most rare.

32. They will be condemned eternally, together with their teachers, who believe themselves sure of their salvation because they have letters of pardon.

33. Men must be on their guard against those who say that the pope's pardons are that inestimable gift of God by which man is reconciled to Him;

34. For these "graces of pardon" concern only the penalties of sacramental satisfaction, and these are appointed by man.

35. They preach no Christian doctrine who teach that contrition is not necessary in those who intend to buy souls out of purgatory or to buy confessionalia.

36. Every truly repentant Christian has a right to full remission of penalty and guilt, even without letters of pardon.

37. Every true Christian, whether living or dead, has part in all the blessings of Christ and the Church; and this is

granted him by God, even without letters of pardon.

38. Nevertheless, the remission and participation [in the blessings of the Church] which are granted by the pope are in no way to be despised, for they are, as I have said, the declaration of divine remission.

39. It is most difficult, even for the very keenest theologians, at one and the same time to commend to the people the abundance of pardons and [the need of] true contrition.

40. True contrition seeks and loves penalties, but liberal pardons only relax penalties and cause them to be hated, or at least, furnish an occasion [for hating them].

41. Apostolic pardons are to be preached with caution, lest the people may falsely think them preferable to other good works of love.

42. Christians are to be taught that the pope does not intend the buying of pardons to be compared in any way to works of mercy.

43. Christians are to be taught that he who gives to the poor or lends to the needy does a better work than buying pardons;

44. Because love grows by works of love, and man becomes better; but by pardons man does not grow better, only more free from penalty.

45. Christians are to be taught that he who sees a man in need, and passes him by, and gives [his money] for pardons, purchases not the indulgences of the pope, but the indignation of God.

46. Christians are to be taught that unless they have more than they need, they are bound to keep back what is necessary for their own families, and by no means to squander it on pardons.

47. Christians are to be taught that the buying of pardons is a matter of free will, and not of commandment.

48. Christians are to be taught that the pope, in granting pardons, needs, and therefore desires, their devout prayer for him more than the money they bring.

49. Christians are to be taught that the pope's pardons are useful, if they do not put their trust in them; but altogether harmful, if through them they lose their fear of God.

50. Christians are to be taught that if the pope knew the exactions of the pardon-preachers, he would rather that St. Peter's church should go to ashes, than that it should be built up with the skin, flesh and bones of his sheep.

51. Christians are to be taught that it would be the pope's wish, as it is his duty, to give of his own money to very many of those from whom certain hawkers of pardons cajole money, even though the church of St. Peter might have to be sold.

52. The assurance of salvation by letters of pardon is vain, even though the commissary, nay, even though the pope himself, were to stake his soul upon it.

53. They are enemies of Christ and of the pope, who bid the Word of God be altogether silent in some Churches, in order that pardons may be preached in others.

54. Injury is done the Word of God when, in the same sermon, an equal or a longer time is spent on pardons than on this Word.

55. It must be the intention of the pope that if pardons, which are a very small thing, are celebrated with one bell, with single processions and ceremonies, then the Gospel, which is the very greatest thing, should be preached with a hundred bells, a hundred processions, a hundred ceremonies.

56. The "treasures of the Church," out of which the pope grants indulgences, are not sufficiently named or known among the people of Christ.

57. That they are not temporal treasures is certainly evident, for many of the vendors do not pour out such treasures so easily, but only gather them.

58. Nor are they the merits of Christ and the Saints, for even without the pope, these always work grace for the inner man, and the cross, death, and hell for the outward man.

59. St. Lawrence said that the treasures of the Church were the Church's poor, but he spoke according to the usage of the word in his own time.

60. Without rashness we say that the keys of the Church, given by Christ's merit, are that treasure;

61. For it is clear that for the remission of penalties and of reserved cases, the power of the pope is of itself sufficient.

62. The true treasure of the Church is the Most Holy Gospel of the glory and the grace of God.

63. But this treasure is naturally most odious, for it makes the first to be last.

64. On the other hand, the treasure of indulgences is naturally most acceptable, for it makes the last to be first.

65. Therefore the treasures of the Gospel are nets with which they formerly were wont to fish for men of riches.

66. The treasures of the indulgences are nets with which they now fish for the riches of men.

67. The indulgences which the preachers cry as the "greatest graces" are known to be truly such, in so far as they promote gain.

68. Yet they are in truth the very smallest graces compared with the grace of God and the piety of the Cross.

69. Bishops and curates are bound to admit the commissaries of apostolic pardons, with all reverence.

70. But still more are they bound to strain all their eyes and attend with all their ears, lest these men preach their own dreams instead of the commission of the pope.

71. He who speaks against the truth of apostolic pardons, let him be anathema and accursed!

72. But he who guards against the lust and license of the pardon-preachers, let him be blessed!

73. The pope justly thunders against those who, by any art, contrive the injury of the traffic in pardons.

74. But much more does he intend to thunder against those who use the pretext of pardons to contrive the injury of holy love and truth.

75. To think the papal pardons so great that they could absolve a man even if he had committed an impossible sin and violated the Mother of God—this is madness.

76. We say, on the contrary, that the papal pardons are not able to remove the very least of venial sins, so far as its guilt is concerned.

77. It is said that even St. Peter, if he were now Pope, could not bestow greater graces; this is blasphemy against St. Peter and against the pope.

78. We say, on the contrary, that even the present pope, and any pope at all, has greater graces at his disposal; to wit, the Gospel, powers, gifts of healing, etc., as it is written in I. Corinthians xii.

79. To say that the cross, emblazoned with the papal arms, which is set up [by the preachers of indulgences], is of equal worth with the Cross of Christ, is blasphemy.

80. The bishops, curates and theologians who allow such talk to be spread among the people, will have an account to render.

81. This unbridled preaching of pardons makes it no easy matter, even for learned men, to rescue the reverence due to the pope from slander, or even from the shrewd questionings of the laity.

82. To wit:—"Why does not the pope empty purgatory, for the sake of holy love and of the dire need of the souls that are there, if he redeems an infinite number of souls for the sake of miserable money with which to build a Church? The former reasons would be most just; the latter is most trivial."

83. Again:—"Why are mortuary and anniversary masses for the dead continued, and why does he not return or permit the withdrawal of the endowments founded on their behalf, since it is wrong to pray for the redeemed?"

84. Again:—"What is this new piety of God and the pope, that for money they allow a man who is impious and their enemy

to buy out of purgatory the pious soul of a friend of God, and do not rather, because of that pious and beloved soul's own need, free it for pure love's sake?"

85. Again:—"Why are the penitential canons long since in actual fact and through disuse abrogated and dead, now satisfied by the granting of indulgences, as though they were still alive and in force?"

86. Again:—"Why does not the pope, whose wealth is to-day greater than the riches of the richest, build just this one church of St. Peter with his own money, rather than with the money of poor believers?"

87. Again:—"What is it that the pope remits, and what participation does he grant to those who, by perfect contrition, have a right to full remission and participation?"

88. Again:—"What greater blessing could come to the Church than if the pope were to do a hundred times a day what he now does once, and bestow on every believer these remissions and participations?"

89. "Since the pope, by his pardons, seeks the salvation of souls rather than money, why does he suspend the indulgences and pardons granted heretofore, since these have equal efficacy?"

90. To repress these arguments and scruples of the laity by force alone, and not to resolve them by giving reasons, is to expose the Church and the pope to the ridicule of their enemies, and to make Christians unhappy.

91. If, therefore, pardons were preached according to the spirit and mind of the pope, all these doubts would be readily resolved; nay, they would not exist.

92. Away, then, with all those prophets who say to the people of Christ, "Peace, peace," and there is no peace!

93. Blessed be all those prophets who say to the people of Christ, "Cross, cross," and there is no cross!

94. Christians are to be exhorted that they be diligent in following Christ, their Head, through penalties, deaths, and hell;

95. And thus be confident of entering into heaven rather through many tribulations, than through the assurance of peace.

ABOUT THE CÁNTARO INSTITUTE

Inheriting, Informing, Inspiring

The Cántaro Institute is a reformed evangelical organization committed to the advancement of the Christian worldview for the reformation and renewal of the church and culture.

We believe that as the Christian church returns to the fount of Scripture as her ultimate authority for all knowing and living, and wisely applies God's truth to every aspect of life, her missiological activity will result in not only the renewal of the human person but also the reformation of culture, an inevitable result when the true scope and nature of the gospel is made known and applied.